DAEDALUS AND ICARUS

DAEDALUS

This great inventor is an architect and an artist … in other words, he has a thousand ideas in his head and builds wonderful toys with great speed! Daedalus comes from the city of Athens, but he is always traveling: His inventions leave everyone speechless. Even kings and queens applaud him and invite him to their palaces. Has someone set a difficult challenge? Is there a problem to be solved? Don't worry, Daedalus helps everyone and can handle any situation. His strokes of genius are foolproof!

ICARUS

Daedalus's son is a curious child who is always on the hunt for adventure. Too bad he's a bit of a rascal.

MINOS

The king of the island of Crete is wise and powerful. But when he gets angry ... best to stay away from him!

PASIPHAE

Minos's beautiful wife is stubborn and courageous, and when she sets her mind to something, she can face any danger.

MINOTAUR

He has the head of a bull and the body of a man, big pointed horns, and long sharp teeth. He is really strong, but unfortunately he has a bad temper.

ENCHANTED GIFTS

TAP TAP

In the palace of King Minos someone is at work with a hammer and nails. It's Daedalus, the world's most famous inventor!

"Are our toys ready?" asks his son Icarus. With him are Ariadne and Glaucus, the king's children. They are very curious and go around touching everything.

"Here are your presents!" exclaims Daedalus. He has built them wooden seahorses and dolls that move on their own. How wonderful!

WATCH OUT FOR THE MINOTAUR!

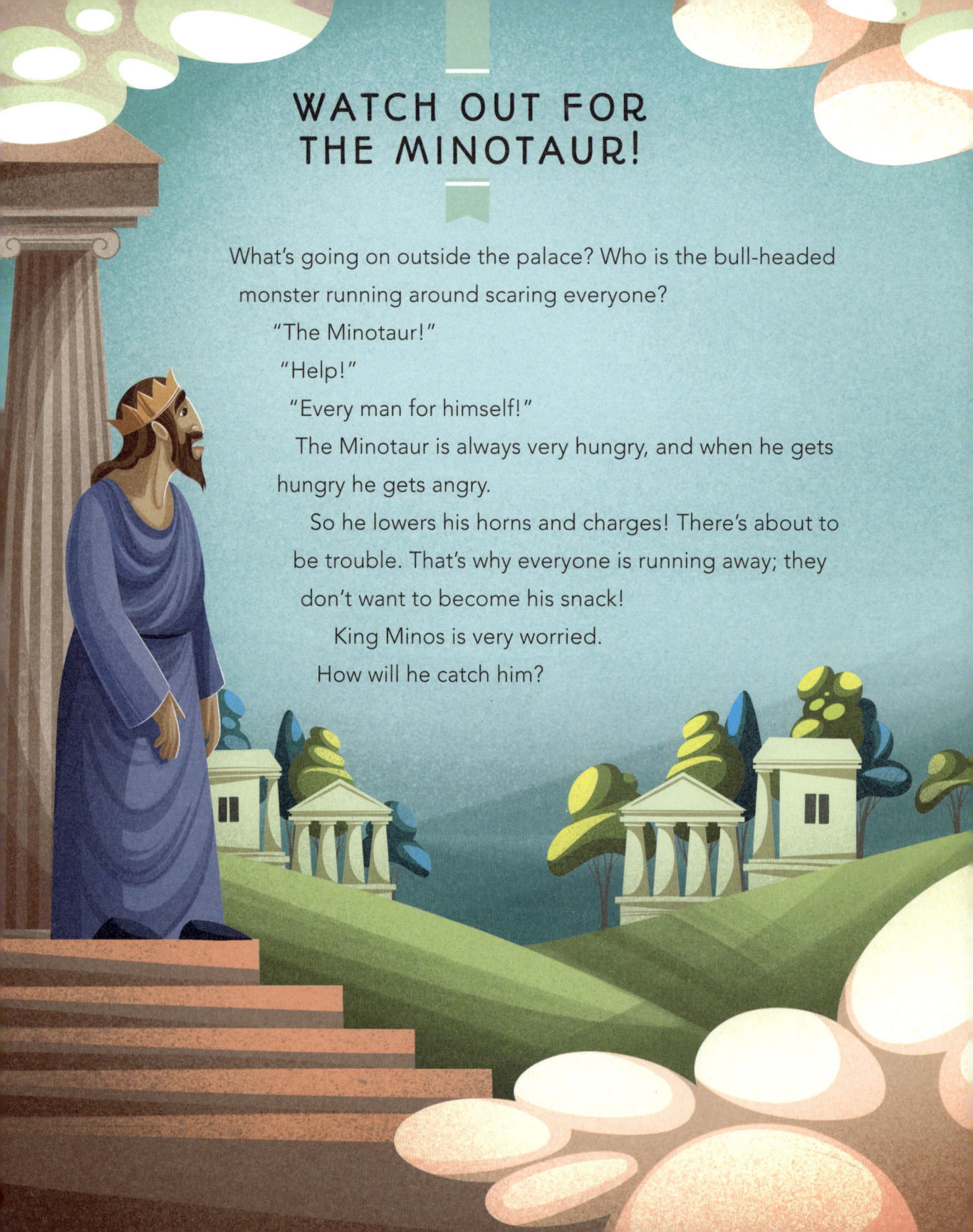

What's going on outside the palace? Who is the bull-headed monster running around scaring everyone?

"The Minotaur!"

"Help!"

"Every man for himself!"

The Minotaur is always very hungry, and when he gets hungry he gets angry.

So he lowers his horns and charges! There's about to be trouble. That's why everyone is running away; they don't want to become his snack!

King Minos is very worried.

How will he catch him?

This requires an ingenious idea! Minos runs to Daedalus. "Will you help me imprison the Minotaur?" he asks him agitatedly.

Daedalus doesn't hesitate. Quickly he sits down at the table and makes lots of drawings. Straight lines, crooked lines, zig-zag lines … this time his design is very complicated.

Finally Daedalus snaps his fingers. "I've got it!" he exclaims happily. "We're going to lock the Minotaur in the Labyrinth so he can't hurt anyone anymore!"

THE LABYRINTH

Minos is overjoyed, but Icarus tugs at his father's arm.

"What is the Labyrinth?" he asks. Daedalus shows him the drawing.

"It will be a huge palace, with more than a thousand rooms. I will build staircases everywhere, secret passages, and even tunnels!"

"Wow! The perfect place to play hide and seek!"

But Daedalus shakes his head. "No, it is too dangerous. The Labyrinth will be so big and intricate that no one will be able to find their way out. Not even the Minotaur!"

MINOS'S ANGRY DECISION

When the Labyrinth is built, the Minotaur is locked inside. Yay!
   Now the monster is a prisoner because only Daedalus can find the exit.
   "Will you tell me the secret?" Ariadne asks him.
   Daedalus is very fond of Minos's sweet daughter, so he teaches her a trick to navigate her way through the Labyrinth. But now the secret is revealed! Minos is very angry with Daedalus and imprisons him along with Icarus … right inside the Labyrinth!

ESCAPE FROM THE LABYRINTH

How dark it is! There are so many noises in the Labyrinth! Long passageways twist in every direction, making their heads spin.

CLACK CLACK CLACK

What's that sound? It's Icarus's teeth chattering in fear.

"King Minos will keep us locked up here forever," he cries. Outside the Labyrinth there are guards everywhere, carefully guarding the exit!

But Daedalus takes his son by the hand. "Don't worry, I have a great idea," he says. "We're going to escape … by flying away!"

TWO PERFECT WINGS

Icarus blinks. "But we don't have wings!" he exclaims.

Daedalus, however, smiles slyly.

"So what? I'll build them," he says. "We just need lots and lots of feathers."

Fortunately, many wild birds fly over the courtyards of the Labyrinth. HOORAY!

Icarus immediately gets to work; he searches for small feathers and big feathers, the feathers of sparrows and of eagles. There are black swallow feathers and white dove feathers.

Will he have enough?

What a beautiful collection! Icarus did a great job.

Now Daedalus can build the wings. First, he chooses the largest feathers and weaves them together. But … OOPS!

The smaller ones won't interwine; they are too short.

"We need wax!" cries Daedalus, running to find some. Icarus softens it with his fingers and together they glue all the small feathers, every last one, with wax.

The two fantastic pairs of wings are ready!

INSTRUCTIONS FOR USE

In the courtyard of the Labyrinth Daedalus ties the wings to Icarus's arms and then puts on his own.

"Be sure not to fly too close to the sun or the feathers will come off," he tells his son. The heat of the sun will melt the wax!

But Icarus isn't listening. He cannot wait to fly away from the Labyrinth and stomps his feet impatiently.

Finally the two begin to run.

They jump, waving their arms quickly.

FLAP FLAP

The great wings lift them gently off their feet.

IN THE AIR!

And suddenly they are flying in the blue sky!

Daedalus and Icarus go higher and higher, much higher than the trees and houses. Grazing sheep look as tiny as ants from up here.

"Look!" cries a shepherd, waving his staff.

"They must be Olympian gods!" the peasants at work in the fields say.

Everyone stares at them open-mouthed.

OOOH!

Daedalus and Icarus fly across the sea, and even the fishermen in their boats pause to turn their faces skyward.

THE MISCHIEF OF ICARUS

Icarus is delighted. He has already learned how the wings work and spins confidently through the sky. He's having so much fun!

He swoops down to skim the sea and then back up again. He makes a left turn, then a right turn. He waves his arms and...

ZOOOM.

The feathers spur him swiftly onward!

Daedalus gives him a warning glance. "Stay close to me," he shouts.

But the boy is already far away and pointing at a little white cloud. Could it be made of milk?

BEWARE OF THE SUN!

Icarus overtakes a flock of seagulls and comes close to touching the cloud.
 These wings really are a marvel! His father Daedalus is the best inventor in the world.
 But suddenly he squints: What is that dazzling light?
 Sunshine.
 Icarus has gone too far, and now it is really hot. He's already all sweaty and...
 DRIP DRIP.
 The wings' wax is melting.

THE WINGS ARE GONE!

A feather falls away and flutters through the sky. Then another and another. What's happening to the wings?

Frightened seagulls fly in circles around Icarus; they want to protect him. Even in the sea, fish jump out of the water to help him.

Be careful Icarus, come back down!

But by now the sun is too close, and its warm rays melt the wax away. AAARGH!

The child waves his arms vigorously, but the wings are gone!

THE ISLAND OF ICARIA

Daedalus turns around, looking for his son ... where has Icarus gone? He's nowhere to be seen.

"Icarus, Icarus," he calls.

But Daedalus is alone in the sky. He looks down and sees feathers floating on the waves.

"I told you not to go near the sun!" he shouts worriedly.

Below is a small island—maybe Icarus is there.

"Now he'll listen!" exclaims Daedalus. "This is what happens when you don't heed my advice!"

And then, opening his wings, he soars down toward the shimmering sea.

Sonia Elisabetta Corvaglia

Sonia Elisabetta Corvaglia was born in the province of Lecce, Italy, and currently lives and works in Milan. She teaches high school literature and collaborates with local libraries as a consultant for projects and workshops to promote literacy and reading. She also oversees school programs to encourage inclusivity and combat bullying, including cyberbullying. She has authored and ghostwritten numerous novels, children's books, and online articles.

Anna Láng

Anna Láng is a Hungarian graphic designer and illustrator who is currently living and working in Sardinia. After attending the Hungarian University of Fine Arts in Budapest, she graduated as a graphic designer in 2011. She was employed for three years at an advertising agency, at the same time working with the National Theatre of Budapest. In 2013, she won the award of the city of Békéscsaba at the Hungarian Biennale of Graphic Design with her Shakespeare Poster series. At present, she is working passionately on illustrations for children's books. In recent years she has brilliantly illustrated a number of titles for White Star Kids.

White Star Kids™ is a trademark of White Star s.r.l.

© 2023 White Star s.r.l.
Piazzale Luigi Cadorna, 6 - 20123 Milan, Italy
www.whitestar.it

Translation: Stephanie Williamson
Editing: Michele Suchomel-Casey

All rights reserved. No part of this publication may be reproduced, stored in a retrieval system, or transmitted in any form or by any means, electronic, mechanical, photocopying, recording, or otherwise, without written permission from the publisher.

First printing, September 2023

ISBN 978-88-544-2029-8
1 2 3 4 5 6   27 26 25 24 23

Printed and manufactured in Turkey by Arkadas Basim San Ltd Sti
Macun Mah.204 Cad. 141/3 Yenimahalle - 06374 Ankara